WORSHIP CRISIS

How to connect with God on a personal level.

Jesse Miller

*For Julie, my amazing wife, Abigial, my creative
daughter, Benjamin, my lively boy, and to
the many people who are part of my journey.
Thank you from the bottom of my heart!*

CONTENTS

CHAPTER 1

Admission

I f you've ever experienced the presence of God in a church service or your prayer closet, you know that it's distinct and unmistakable. It's not some euphoric feeling pulsing through you because the electric guitarist is playing some Slash inspired riff, it's the Holy Spirit manifesting the power of God. Nothing compares to it because it's not a feeling but an encounter that's marked by peace that could only come from on high.

I have led worship for 25 years at churches, youth groups, missions' trips to foreign countries, conventions, conferences, and more. I have been in the church far more than most people I know, and I love the presence of God. But there have been many times when I could tell the presence of God was in the room, but I felt nothing. No emotion. No connection to God's Presence. People would tell me how much a song had ministered to them, or how much a line from my preaching meant to them, but I felt nothing.

When I started digging into my lack of fulfillment in times of worship, I found some answers from the Bible that set me free. I realized that my problem was due in part to my addiction to worship music. So, let me start by getting something off my chest:

Hi, my name is Jesse, and I'm a worshipholic. It's been three days since my last service.

"Hi, Jesse."

One of the basic tenets of AA doctrine is to admit you have a problem. But we've been conditioned to say everything is ok. Societal norms say to be polite at the expense of being mended. It's ingrained in us to say we're 'doing good' when someone asks us how we're doing. We trade pleasantries rather than speaking our mind. But we also ask people how they're doing without wanting to know the real answer. That's because the real answer is messy. It's harder to deal with the truth.

As we dig into the Word of God, you may find that your worship time isn't as magical as you think. You may even discover, as I did, that you have a worship problem. And let me give you a hint – the problem isn't with God.

We are living in the greatest age for worship music since the foundation of the world. If you like hymns, they're still here. You want some Country worship? You can have it. Rock? Pop? Jazz? If you can think of a style of worship available for you to connect to the Almighty, it's available as quickly as you can type. So even though your church may not play the style you like, it's still available for your devotion time.

On top of this, the fog, light shows, soaring guitars, thick layered synths, and processed drums rival anything coming out of mainstream Nashville. Of course, if you prefer a pipe organ and a choir, that's still available. So, you have the greatest choice of styles and songs today that you ever had in the course of human history, and you can listen to it at any time. It would stand to reason that the people alive on the earth today, at this very minute, would be the happiest, most connected Christians to the Creator that have ever lived. But still, there is a problem.

The problem isn't new.

It affects everyone.

It won't resolve on this side of Heaven.

But you can identify it.

You can get the victory over it.

And it all started with amazing fruit.

Any good detective worth his salt would tell you that when you're questioning a suspect, you get a statement, asking them to start at the beginning and tell what happened. I pulled on my investigative journalism hat and got to work. What's amazing is, out of 1,189 chapters in the Bible, it only took until Genesis 3 to find the first instance of this problem.

Before we look at the problem, let's start with the ultimate and original desire of God.

Genesis 1:26-28 NKJV "Then God said, 'Let Us make man in Our image, according to Our likeness; let them have dominion over the fish of the sea, over the birds of the air, and over the cattle, over all the earth and over every creeping thing that creeps on the earth.' So God created man in His own image; in the image of God He created him; male and female He created them. Then God blessed them, and God said to them, 'Be fruitful and multiply; fill the earth and subdue it; have dominion over the fish of the sea, over the birds of the air, and over every living thing that moves on the earth.'"

God made us in His image. If you want to know what God looks like, then look in a mirror. He designed you and me to look like Him. It wasn't a stretch for the Son of God to come to earth as a human. His features and likeness would have been similar to his features and likeness in Heaven. It's only a stretch to our brain because we see our flaws, and our flab, and our imperfections and wonder why we aren't perfect. It's because we measure things through our knowledge of good and evil lens, rather than the lens of innocence.

But it's not just our faces or our bodies. It's also our personality. The root Hebrew word for likeness is demuth, which means resemblance, like manner, and similitude. Kind of like the Transformers, there's more to you than meets the eye. Your laugh and smile reflect God. Your sense of wonder and adventure are part of the fabric of your being that were created by God. Our anger, tear, and disappointments are traits and part of the likeness that we have received from the Lord. If that messes with your theology, then please keep reading because we will address this throughout the book.

Unless you can begin to understand the planning, the thought, the care, and the painstakingly intricate details that God went through to create you, then times of worship and communion with God will stay distant and aloof. His created beings, it's our great pleasure to discover this so we can move into a deep and meaningful relationship with the Master Artisan. Every good parent can remember the first time they held their child in their arms, and they saw the little life made in their likeness and their image. We inherited that feeling from our Father God because it's the feeling He had when He saw His first man and woman that He had created.

In her poem, Human Family, Maya Angelou sums this thought up when she states, "I note the obvious differences between each sort and type, but we are more alike, my friends, than we are un-alike.

If we can change our mindset to see how we have the life, the nature, and the essence of His per-sonality weaved into our hearts and souls, we will make great strides towards turning into the people God intended us to be. And He could have made us love Him. God could have forced us to honor and love Him. But we all know that forced love isn't real. And we serve a God of truth, so it's not in His nature to do that.

If it weren't for the ability to choose, we would all still be in the garden of Eden, naked as a jaybird, and not knowing any better. If it weren't for free will, the devil and his angels would still be in Heaven playing beautiful music. There would be no wars, no violence, no fighting because every-one would be programmed to do everything com-manded in the Bible. It always sounds good on paper, but imagine making that into a plot for a movie:

"In a perfect world lived a man. He woke up on time every day and went to a perfect job for which he was perfectly suited. He married the perfect per-son, and they had a perfect life with no problems.

No one ever fought or argued. No one ever had problems because they were programmed perfectly. Also, no one died because everything was perfect."

What a dull movie that would be! What a boring premise. That's because plotlines of movies rise and fall on conflict. No one wants to watch a movie about a perfect person because it's predictable. There's no emotion or heart in it. It's devoid of everything that makes us human with a free will.

Do you know how much freedom that God granted us at our creation? Look at the power he gave Adam:

Genesis 2:19 NKJV ^{Out} of the ground the Lord God formed every beast of the field and every bird of the air, and brought them to Adam to see what he would call them. And whatever Adam called each living creature, that was its name.

One of the first things God does is bring the animals to Adam to see what he would name them. He gave him dominion over everything in the earth and made him the steward of the Garden of Eden. God delighted in seeing what Adam would do with his free will.

Then something happened.

Free will created a Free Willy sized rift between God and man.

Human death entered the world.

I'm sure even if you're not a regular church attender, somewhere along the way, you have heard the story of how the serpent tricked Eve into eating fruit from the tree of knowledge of good and evil. And of course, Adam ate the fruit as well, so he was complicit in the disobedience to God's command.

It would be easy to point the finger at sin and blame disobedience as the root cause of our problems with worship. We could make the argument that spiritual death that caused our separation from God is the primary source of our problems. But as I looked closer at both the evidence from scripture and the evidence in nature of how parents interact with their children, I came to form a different opinion. This problem is the heart of the issue and the premise for this book. Let's look at Genesis 3:8 NKJV:

"And they heard the sound of the Lord God walking in the garden in the cool of the day, and Adam and his wife hid themselves from the presence of the Lord God among the trees of the garden."

The problem with worship is hiding.

When I realized that I hindered my worship because I was either knowingly or unknowingly hiding things from God in my communion with Him, it was an epic moment for me personally! The light bulb came on, and my thoughts and intents were laid bare before the Lord. As I dealt with my heart's secrets, God revealed Himself to me in a way I had not experienced in a long time.

It's easy to look at this passage and focus on the commands God gave to Adam and Eve not to eat from the tree. It's easy to focus on the consequences given to Adam and Eve after they disobeyed. But I think the most profound thing in this passage is uncovering this problem of hiding.

When I was a kid, we played the age-old game of hide and seek. It didn't matter if you were the hider or seeker – the fun part was when you found someone. If you were hiding and someone found you, it was fun because you became the seeker. The game stopped being fun when someone was so good that no one could find them. Or they cheated and hid across the street in the Williams house. And Mrs. Williams was a willing accomplice to this treasonous act. Especially when your mother wouldn't do anything about your cheating brother's secret stowaway spot. But I digress...

Being hidden with Christ in God is not the same as hiding from God. There are plenty of places that speak of safety and security in the arms of God. There's even a Psalm (91:4) that says He will cover us with His feathers, and under His wings we will take refuge. Hiding in God is a completely different matter.

I'm so glad you're still reading this book because I want to show you the journey I went on through the scriptures and my own experiences that have reignited my times of worship, and have made the Word come alive again in my heart!

CHAPTER 2

Despair

After five years of pastoring a church plant, I felt that God had called me to, I knew it was time to release the people and myself to pursue other ministries. To use the word drained would be an understatement. I tried everything I knew to do – mail flyers, go door-to-door, give away things in the mall, post on social media, and much more! What's weird about it was that even though our church never took off, God blessed me so much in the secular world that I was making more money than I ever thought possible. As Charles Dickens said in A Tale of Two Cities, "It was the best of times, it was the worst of times..."

I was at my lowest point. I felt like I had failed even though my wife and I had separately heard the Lord speak to our hearts to go to San Diego. It's not like God didn't move in our little congregation at all – we had people come and get saved, healed, and set free from addictions. Why didn't it stick? Why didn't God answer my prayers? How could I be a pastor, yet feel like I was dead inside?

I'm sure you've never felt this way – I know you're perfect and have never felt abandoned by God – I'm just talking about myself.

It was the Summer of 2016 and felt like a zombie living in my host body. I just wanted to attend church. I said, "Well, God is blessing my marketplace ministry, so this must be my new calling." The funny thing about God is that when He gives you a gift or a calling, He's not apologetic about it, and he doesn't say, "Oops, I changed my mind…" With God, there's no backsies.

The simple answer for my failure in ministry was the same reason I languished in my soul. Rather than deal with little setbacks or unsuccessful attempts at growth, I hid my feelings away because this "man of faith" couldn't be seen as weak. My path to burnout and self-loathing led me to dread looking at social media or read the latest magazine that contained the list of the 100 fastest growing churches in America.

Don't misunderstand – I tried with every fiber of my being to rejoice with the victories of other churches. We made it a point to locate all the churches in a 5-mile radius of the church and pray for a different ministry each week. Then we sent that church a note telling them we had prayed for them, and that we weren't in competition but wanted the best for them and their ministries. I suppressed covetousness and enviousness with my whole heart. No, there was something else at work, and the sins of coveting thy neighbor's church were just the evil cousins.

My wife says I do a good job at hiding what I think and feel with my facial expressions. I tell her that she does a terrible job and that I would like to play her in poker and take all her money. Possessing a poker face might be a blessing while playing poker or for when a lawyer interrogates you on the witness stand, but what about your relationships with your family? What about your relationship with God?

Here's a Jesse Miller quote for you: "A smile can cover a multitude of hurts." We don't need to bring up the slew of recent comedians who have committed suicide to know that there's more to the show than the laughter. We say things like, "this too shall pass," or some other trite expression, and we celebrate the guy with the poker face or the girl who's always happy.

God has given us such complex emotions and feelings that like Joy in the movie Inside Out, we try to keep every memory happy, and every moment upbeat, and we try to suppress our sadness, our feelings of failure of guilt. Of course, we blame this on the Lord by incorrectly thinking that we have a destiny of happiness that includes floating around on a cloud all the time. That couldn't be further from the truth.

I remember looking at my wife after our last

Sunday with our congregation in August of 2016 and asking her what I did wrong. Our goal was to create a Chain Reaction of God's love in the city of San Diego that would spread throughout the town and to the world. Our mission was to find lost and hurting people and pray for them and build them up and encourage them. We wanted to give food to the hungry, establish a network with other pastors in town, and effect real change in the city. Our intentions were noble.

It was months before I began to even breakthrough in my prayer time with God because of all the suppressed emotions I felt. I said to the Lord, "God, I just saw another stupid TV preacher who has more money than she knows what to do with telling people that if they gave $145.15 based on Psalm 145:15 that supernatural debt relief would come to them. Lord, there's not one scripture in the Bible that tells us to preach that, and its heresy. I can't believe they are spouting off nonsense. Yet they have a big ministry and a big following. I just wanted to start a church to help hurting people, and I failed. Why are you blessing them, and not me?"

Some of you PhDs out there may have it all figured out, and you're punching holes in my flawed theology, but the truth is, I was finally getting honest with God. After over 30 years of walking with the Lord, my relationship with God had gone from 20-30 prayers, I prayed regularly to a couple hundred, but I was still in a rut. I was hiding behind my phrases and expressions. Sure, my Christian vocabulary and knowledge of the Word had grown, but I found myself going through a shopping list of the stuff I should say to God in prayer to get certain results, rather than baring my soul before Him.

You will never be free in hiding. I was not free. The reason I went into hiding is because of the fear of being exposed. The best hiding spaces are usually dark and quiet. And for someone with a poker face, you can hide in plain sight even though it's dark and quiet – right inside your mind.

It's a funny thing – we think we can hide from the Lord, but scripture tells us otherwise. When King David wrote Psalm 139, he exposed this truth. In verses 7-10 NKJV, it says:

Where can I go from Your Spirit?
Or where can I flee from Your presence?
If I ascend into heaven, You are there;
If I make my bed in hell, behold, You are there.
If I take the wings of the morning,
And dwell in the uttermost parts of the sea,
Even there Your hand shall lead me,
And Your right hand shall hold me.

And in Hebrews 4:13 NKJV: And there is no creature hidden from His sight, but all things are naked and open to the eyes of Him to whom we must give account.

There's no escaping. There's nowhere to run or hide. And that would be horrible if we were talking about the devil, but we are talking about the One who made us special and unique — the One who knows every hair on our heads. We are talking about the Grand Architect of this beautiful universe. We're talking about our Good, Good Father.

So here I sat, complaining to God about me, me, me. And He waited patiently. But I kept talking. Finally, when I stayed quiet long enough, I felt like these words rose in my spirit: "I called you into the ministry, but your ministry does not define who you are."

Sometimes when someone shares the revelation that God gave them, it doesn't have the same effect on other people. It's because God revealed it to them, and not you. So, let me try and explain why this is significant.

Up until our church plant, I had been successful. God allowed me to lead worship and play the keyboard at events like Promise Keepers, March for Jesus, our youth group as a teen, a 5,000-member church, and at several churches where I was on staff. I even led worship for other teenage missionaries for a summer in Russia. Many doors opened to me. I could have taken over as Senior Pastor of the last place I served in the Youth Pastor role. Everything was moving in the right direction.

After a moving message or a great worship event, people would come up to me and tell me all kinds of flattering things. It was sincere and heartfelt. And when I was experiencing success, I began linking the two together. Words of affirmation = successful ministry.

Except, when my wife and I planted the church in San Diego, people were still saying kind and flattering things, but we weren't growing. We ministered to many people, but I had to pray in enough money to continue to pay the rent for the building. The songs I was singing and the Word I was preaching had not changed, but now the success was not there. The kind words did not equal fruit in kind.

As this continued throughout the five years, bitterness rose in my heart, and I began to think I had no anointing. I began to believe that God didn't call me to the ministry. But that couldn't be right because Romans 11:29 in the Amplified Version says, "For God's gifts and His call are irrevocable. [He never withdraws them when once they are given, and He does not change His mind about those to whom He gives His grace or to whom He sends His call.]

Isn't it always easier to look back and pinpoint what went wrong? It's glaringly obvious now that I built a wall between myself and God, and myself and others. The longer time marched on, and my church didn't grow, I began to sink into a depression that I blamed on my failure.

When depression takes hold, it doesn't care about the reasons behind why it happens; it just takes joy in wallowing in the sacred mud of self-pity. The root of depression lives in that arena of not getting what you felt you deserved. It wraps its tentacles around your heart and tells you that no one loves you, that the world is out to get you, and nothing you do will get you out of this funk. The only hope it offers is that you can set up a wall and begin to feel sorry for yourself.

Now there is a disease of depression which involves an imbalance in your brain because of lack of certain chemicals that just aren't flowing right. But for most depressed people, life has beaten them down, knocked them in a hole, and offered no rope to pull themselves out. And because of the weak state a person would find themselves in at that moment, they shut out the answers and the solutions to their problems, namely God, family, and friends. You may not be in a state of full-blown depression, but there are experiences in every person's life that cause them to retreat and pull back or go into hiding. Or, at the very least, in the area of their life, they're struggling in.

Social media has created a completely different culture where we post the great things and leave out the bad. There are "influencers" that live in mansions together, and they receive huge sums of money to make videos detailing all the best parts of their lives. Others make lots of money, creating fake drama. But that's the crux of it – it's fake.

You may wonder what all of this has to do with worship. It has everything to do with our relationship with God. If there are parts of you that are not accessible to God and the world, then it will stunt your relational growth. We can't get closer to anyone if we build a foxhole and bunker down. If you begin to feel distant from God in your times of worship, remember that He's not the one that moved.

It's easy to recognize there is a problem. When

two people are dating, walls and layers come down as they get closer. There are good reasons why those walls and layers went up in the first place, but the more those two people trust each other, the more they reveal. As time continues to march on in that relationship, the couple either falls more in love, even knowing all the hurts and bruises, scars, and imperfections, or they drift apart. It's usually not a surprise either way. Either you have a diamond, or you have coal dust.

If your relationship with God has become rocky, and you feel like He's in a galaxy far, far away, the good news is that you have determined that there's a problem in your relationship. And the very fact that you want to patch things up is even better news! Remember, you picked up and started reading a book called "The Problem with Worship." Or maybe you're listening to the audiobook. Either way, you most likely are struggling in some area of your connection with the Master. That's ok! Don't throw in the towel. Don't give up on this relationship. God never moved away from you or changed His mind about you.

The Holy Spirit is drawing you.

Jesus paid for this communion with His very own blood.

You are worth it.

And if you stick around, I want to show you actions that I took to reignite the fire by looking at the lives and lyrics of men and women of old that went through the same problems and feelings that we all experience. There is light at the end of this tunnel!

CHAPTER 3

Light

In his book, "Death by A Thousand Lies," Blaine Bartel reveals several powerful truths he learned when he went through his dark night of the soul. This one stuck with me:

Jesus was not afraid of Lazarus's stink, and he's not afraid of ours. He just rolls away the stone of our foul, reeking tomb and calls for the life of God to resurrect our aching soul.

Sin is foul. It is humiliating and scandalous. But it is precisely why Jesus stepped into death on Good Friday and burst back to life on Easter Sunday!

Blaine had been a very influential minister in my life as a teenager. His program targeted to youth, Fire by Night, was a great source of the latest music, Christian humor, and Biblical advice on relevant topics for teens. I looked forward to the VHS tape each month that arrived at our church library. Then, after graduating Bible College and becoming a youth pastor, I turned to his ministry Oneighty at Church on the Move in Tulsa, OK, for more tips and tricks to build an epic youth program at my church. I looked up to him because he was doing all the things I wanted to do myself.

My heart languished to find that he had carried a secret 25-year addiction to pornography, prostitutes, and all kinds of sexual depravity. When the truth came out, I remember instantly judging him and asking God why He used this man for so long in such a public ministry, while he was dealing with this issue the entire time. Of course, in my prayer time, the Holy Spirit brought this verse to my memory:

Matthew 7:1-2 NLT Do not judge others, and you will not be judged. For you will be treated as you treat others. The standard you use in judging is the standard by which you will be judged.

Look, Blaine was wrong. What he did was wrong on so many levels. And he wrote a confessional book, sparing no details of his depravity. But he has asked the Lord to forgive him, and we are either going to believe that God forgave him, or we will continue to judge him. Either way, our decisions to forgive him or not forgive only affect us. Trust me, if he is truly penitent, his largest obstacle for the rest of his life will be to live in God's forgiveness of his sin, not the judgment from strangers with their problems.

When God chose Saul to be the first king of Israel after they rejected the Lord having the rule over them, they had trouble finding him. I like the way it reads in the KJV, "Behold he hath hid himself among the stuff." So, the Lord had picked a tall man who was head and shoulders above the other people, and he was humble, modest, and not desirous of the position.

But when we skip forward a few years, we have a different man before us. God spoke through the prophet Samuel that King Saul was to destroy everything in the town of Amalek. Men. Women. Children. Sheep. Camels. Donkeys. Everything. The commandment was very clear.

King Saul, the King of Hide and Seek, already had an answer prepared. He said to Samuel the Prophet, "May you be blessed by the Lord; I have carried out the command of the Lord." 1 Samuel 15:13 NRSV

However, if you study this story out, the truth rears its ugly head. The Lord had already revealed to Samuel that Saul had not done what was commanded. God was regretful that He had ever made Saul the King of Israel. It was on this day that Saul was rejected by God to remain king.

I think the real question in this story is, what went wrong? Doesn't God forgive? Why didn't God reject Noah, or Abraham, or King David when they all sinned and did wrong?

There is an eerily similar scenario between Adam and Eve and King Saul. First, they both hid their revelations of wrongdoing. Second, they placed blame on others. If you are feeling distant in your times of worship, is there something that you are hiding from God or from people that should know? Or is the blame for your problems shifting to other people or even God? Human nature has remained constant from Adam and Eve until now. The idea that we could hide anything from God is laughable, and most of the time, other people find out about the secrets we have hidden. But we continue to hide.

Getting back to my story, the things I buried deep in my soul were feelings of jealousy and envy towards successful ministries. I felt shame for failing to get a church off the ground that I felt was instructed by the Lord. I felt like I had given up a good job at a good church with a great pastor to trudge through a church plant without a good backing. I constantly hated working a secular job out of necessity to plant the church. And I was angry that I gave up a good job in a good church doing what I loved full-time.

You may have a different story, but I'm sure if you ask the Lord to reveal areas of your life that are off-limits to Him, He will. God never uncovers us to shame us; he uncovers us to heal us. He takes our heart of stone and gives us a heart of flesh. What are areas of your life closed off to discuss with your loved ones? Did you get passed over for a job or promotion? Did your High School coach not use your talents enough? Did you get rejected by someone that you loved deeply? Are there hurts and pains that you have placed a Band-Aid on, but you keep picking at the scab and wondering why it won't heal? There are myriad of things that you are embarrassed about or things that trigger a feeling of shame. But there are also many things for which you feel shame, yet you have done nothing wrong.

My wife, who is a wonderful mother, who loves our kids with all her heart, is constantly wondering if she has spent enough time with them or done enough for them. She worries about their well-being and welfare and wants them to have the most opportunities to succeed in everything they do. She has no reason to feel shame, yet she does. She hasn't done anything wrong, but she thinks she has.

If you're a mother, you may share these same feelings and emotions. You may feel guilt and shame for absolutely no reason at all. There is no big sin in your life that has separated you from God, but you feel guilty for things you haven't done. Guilt and shame are 2 of the biggest liars you will find. If the devil thinks there's a chance that he can get to you by making you feel guilty for something you haven't done, he's happy with that because when guilt and shame grip you, it rips you apart just as much as if you had done something wrong. That's because you're still applying the same emotional response to something that isn't something, as you would to something that is. It is just as damaging.

Some people have seared their consciences to the point where they feel no shame for their wrong-doings. They walk around appearing to those around them to be freer and more liberated because they have not applied guilt and shame to their sin. And of course, the devil never will – they are walking into the trap he has laid out for them. The fact that no remorse exists doesn't excuse the sin, make it right, or free them from any consequences, but it can give them temporary relief from pending eternal suffering. I don't mean to be dark here, but the Bible clearly says that the wages of sin is death. The path is dark but thank God that he can free anyone from this problem!

By now, I'm sure you're beginning to see that there are many ways we find ourselves distant from God. It could be something we've done that brings conviction. Or it could be some fake guilt and shame that is being held over us by our adversary, the devil. Although we could list many more, let's focus on one other reason that plagues many people, especially in modern, developed nations.

Exhaustion.

Yes, while taking kids to sporting events, volunteering for this thing and that, working overtime to pay for all these things and then trying to squeeze in some time for the Most High, many people are constantly living at their breaking point. They have succeeded in obtaining everything they ever dreamed of, but they are too tired to appreciate it and too busy to enjoy the fruits of their labor. You're not learning anything new here – this problem has been ongoing for generations.

Once again, there are plenty of books of cautionary tales to take time and smell the roses. Cat's in the Cradle is always playing on some radio station around Father's Day. Scrooge's treatment of Bob Cratchit is an indictment of employers mishandling their employees that has lasted in literature and film for nearly 200 years. The book Boundaries by Dr. Henry Cloud and Dr. John Townsend is an excellent read that empowers readers to understand how to limit themselves and learn to say no. I'm sure you can think of many books, tv episodes, or advice you have received on the importance of slowing down, so life doesn't pass in the blink of an eye.

From the scriptures, we have the great example of sisters Martha and Mary who both loved the Lord, but had differing priorities:

Luke 10:38-42 NLT says, 'As Jesus and the disciples continued on their way to Jerusalem, they came to a certain village where a woman named Martha welcomed him into her home. Her sister, Mary, sat at the Lord's feet, listening to what he taught. But Martha was distracted by the big dinner she was preparing. She came to Jesus and said, "Lord, doesn't it seem unfair to you that my sister sits here while I do all the work? Tell her to come and help me."

But the Lord said to her, "My dear Martha, you are worried and upset over all these details! There is only one thing worth being concerned about. Mary has discovered it, and it will not be taken away from her."'

What I find significant in this story is that it's Martha's house. She invited Jesus to her house. It was her party. No problem existed until Martha complained about Mary to Jesus. Sometimes our exhaustion stems from being busy in well-doing but missing the point. She had the Lamb of God in her house, and she was distracted by lamb chops.

We have the best plans for our children, but we work into the night to provide money for them when they need love and attention. We volunteer for their activities but are exhausted from the extra work it takes to get ready for those activities. We get involved in helping at church, but because we are too nice to say no, we end up being the first one there, the last to leave, and we eventually burn out.

In my situation, I found myself in the heart of San Diego, trying to start a church to reach out to the lost, the forgotten, and the broken. I even found a job with a four-day work week installing cable tv. My hopes were high, and my excitement was growing to plant a thriving, vibrant ministry in the city. However, it wasn't long until my four-day week stretched to 5, then six mandatory days. I was logging 70 hours some of those weeks. It was all I could do to scrape together the energy to get a message together, and the worship set. It fell upon my family to load up the sound system, the children's ministry, hang the banner, and meet me at the elementary school at 5:30 pm on Sunday nights, half an hour before our service was to start. To say I was an exhausted heap of mess would have been an understatement.

I kept telling myself that it was just for a season. And while there may be truth to that, it was not sustainable. I don't care if you're Billy Graham, or Leonard Ravenhill, or Dwight Moody, there's no way you can accurately and passionately pastor a church when you are physically, emotionally and spiritually drained from working a secular job 70 hours a week. Even if you get people to start coming, you have no time for them because you are not available to them throughout the week at all. If they just wanted to hear preaching or music, they could go to YouTube or Apple Music. The people we were trying to reach didn't need a Sunday sermonette; they needed a pastor who would be there with them in the trenches of battle. They needed someone who could walk with them through the problems of life. I had enough problems on my own at this point.

While my failures as a church planter may not resonate strongly with you, perhaps the feeling of exhaustion will. And it seems that when the cares of life lift their ugly heads, they are more than happy to squeeze out your time of Bible Study and prayer first. Somehow, it becomes easy to justify your actions because you're working to provide for your family, and easy to let the one thing that will provide life and nourishment for your spirit and soul fall away. The great trick that the devil uses in our culture is this: keep the troops busy, so they won't have time for Bible study, prayer, reflection, meditation, fasting, or quality time with their loved ones.

Doing the work of the ministry can create burnout for some people. Just like Martha, it's easy to justify neglecting our families in the name of advancing the Kingdom. Many times, Martha gets a bad rap, but she loved the Lord. In her mind, getting that food ready was more important than sitting at the Master's feet. But Jesus desired her soul, not her soul food. There is nothing more important in life than sitting at the feet of the Master and allowing Him to speak to you.

Don't get offended at what I'm going to say next. God is not impressed that you climbed the corporate ladder and became the CEO of a multi-national corporation. God is not impressed that you rescued 200 orphans from sex-trafficking and raised them yourself. God is not impressed by your accolades, even if you did them for Him. It may be hard to hear, but if we're going to improve our relationship with God, we must get to the bottom of the problem, and it may be the tough love that finally frees you. And for this tough love, let's find out what Jesus said in conclusion to His Sermon on the Mount:

Matthew 7:21-23 NKJV "Not everyone who says to Me, 'Lord, Lord,' shall enter the kingdom of heaven, but he who does the will of My Father in heaven. Many will say to Me in that day, 'Lord,

Lord, have we not prophesied in Your name, cast out demons in Your name, and done many wonders in Your name?' And then I will declare to them, 'I never knew you; depart from Me, you who practice lawlessness!'

As much as we want to feel God's presence, and have an emotionally stimulating relationship with God, anyone who is a student of the Bible knows that feeling emotional towards God doesn't create a salvation experience. Not even reading the Bible will put us in right-standing with Him. The only thing that moves God is our faith.

It's an evil trick that the enemy uses to make us think that anything other than faith would deepen our relationship with Him. We may be from different denominational backgrounds, and we may differ on some of the finer points of doctrine, but the common thread that must bind together all true Christian churches is Jesus. And the way to Heaven is by accepting that we are a sinner, believing that Jesus died and rose again from the grave, then confessing with our mouth that Jesus is Lord. This truth is something that we hold as a basic tenant of faith.

So why in the world would we hold up our achievements to God and think that the more we do for Him, the more impressed He will be in us? How did we get to the point that our closeness to God has anything to do with that? We even sing songs with words like, "I will praise you in the storm..." or "I will praise you in the valleys all the same."

By thinking that God is impressed with our accomplishments, we wrongly assume that the mountaintop experiences are most valuable. That means that when a true valley comes to our life – loss of a job, loved one, severe illness, fill in the blank, that we associate this time with God not being pleased with us, and therefore giving us the silent treatment. This misunderstanding couldn't be further from the truth!

At the time of this writing, I have professed Jesus as my Savior for 34 years. I have been to Bible School, and I know the Word. However, when my church plant didn't succeed, it wrecked me to my core. I may have known what the Word said about this, but I wasn't acting on it. Instead, I allowed the bitterness, and my feelings of loneliness and despair creep in my heart. I associated the church plant failure with God not being pleased with me. Somehow because I didn't succeed at this, I did something to anger God. I was in the valley, so I figured I would lay there and wallow in the mud.

Until...

I let in the light.

I began to listen.

I allowed the healing to come.

As I said earlier in this book, it was at this point where God said to me in my spirit: "I called you into the ministry, but your ministry does not define who you are."

This revelation shined light into the dark crevasses of my heart. Calling the Christian life a walk of faith was not a trite expression but the truth. My feelings were not allowed to dictate who I was. My success or failure had no right to determine my position with Christ. Either I was in right relationship with God or not. Either I would believe what the Word said, or I would trust my feelings. Either God loves me, or he doesn't.

You see, the difference at that moment was not whether I felt close to God or not, the difference is I began to view my relationship with the Father through the Word rather than what I felt in the valley. If Paul said in Ephesians 2:6 that we have been raised with Christ and seated with Him in the Heavenly Realms, then either Paul lied, or he wrote down what God told him to write. We can't say we believe the Word of God is infallible, then blame Him for the problems we are experiencing. Sure, God can handle it when we reject Him and His commandments, but can we?

Our relationship with God the Father hinges on faith. Our relationship with Jesus Christ, who walked the earth 2,000 years ago before video cameras and satellite television, is based on faith. Our relationship with the Holy Spirit, our Comforter and Guide, and Helper relies on faith. When we can get to the point where we trust God the way Abraham trusted God with his son Isaac, we can experience the healing love that He brings.

The way I experienced emotional healing, and spiritual restoration was by changing my heart from Martha to Mary. I sat at the Lord's feet and re-learned the doctrine I eschewed from the pulpit for many years. I sat in service as a congregation member and allowed God's healing power to wash over me during the times of worship and preaching. I stopped trying to be something and just became myself.

By all means, preach the Gospel in every continent to every people group! By all means, grow a huge corporation that employs thousands and fund the spread of the Gospel. By all means, rescue kids from sex trafficking and all kinds of perversions, and teach them about Jesus. But don't do any of it at the expense of your relationship with God or your family. It's not worth it. We have a lot of important work to do on this earth, but there is nothing more important than your relationship with the Lord.

CHAPTER 4

Conviction

By now, I hope you can agree with me that the problem with worship isn't on God's side! And while it's important to get to the bottom of why we have problems in our times of worship, it's also not Biblical or helpful to assign the blame to those things. Blame and shame only further the cause of the enemy. No, in the courts of Heaven, we see God sending Jesus to the world to convict of sin for repentance. And conviction is another thing entirely than condemnation.

When I was a youth pastor in Missouri, we would take trips to concerts, events, camps, and much more. It was a lot of fun! And often, I would have a stash of cash from the last-minute payers that I would have to keep track of for the weekend until we arrived back at church. I'll never forget the time I bought a concert t-shirt for myself out of that stack of cash. What a miserable idea that turned out to be. Of course, my flesh justified it by saying, "You are making $200 per week as a full-time youth pastor. You deserve to get a little reward for your efforts." But from the moment I did that, I was convicted. I knew it was wrong. God wasn't torturing me; it was my conscience. It was that voice that God put inside of every person referenced at the end of Romans 1, where we instinctively know what God wants us to do, so we are without excuse. This annoyingly loud alarm was sounding in my head, and the moment I received my next paycheck, I added the $20 for the t-shirt to my tithes and offerings. Immediately it subsided, and peace returned.

I didn't feel shame or condemnation – I allowed the Holy Spirit to convict my heart. It was a matter of doing the right thing. It was the heart of Achan rising when the whole time I knew the spoils were in my tent. Nothing stops our worship more than ignoring convictions that come from the Holy Spirit. We ask the Holy Spirit to come with us, be our guide, be our helper until we don't want Him to be there anymore because we feel the holy nudge to go the other way. In the same way that Jonah received no rest until he arrived in Nineveh to preach repentance to the people, a true disciple of Jesus with a heart to do good and do right will want to know the right way to go.

But there's a problem.

We don't like conviction. We don't like confrontation with things we need to change. All the men reading this will agree that we don't like giving up control of even the remote in the house because it may require us to watch a program we have no desire to see. In my house, this means that either I will be watching Paw Patrol with the kids, or Women's College Basketball with my wife.

The simple truth is – it's easier to go into hiding than it is to stand and conquer our fears and vices. However, when you look at the many examples in scripture, in human nature, and when you examine your own heart, it's easy to conclude that hiding is the main obstacle to our communication with God. That may not be true of everyone. I mean, have you looked at Facebook lately? Some people don't mind spilling their innermost thoughts and failures for the world to see. But for many, they would rather have their friends and Social Media buddies only see the good side of their lives.

Is the answer to vomit all your problems and fears over your family and friends? Hardly! Is there a 12-step program to pull you out of your funk? Maybe. What about a Christian Counselor – I heard they could be helpful? Somewhat.

The truth is the silver bullet that exists to resurrect you and breathe life into your dry bones and weary soul is simple to understand but difficult to master. Rather than give you a simple definition, the following story describes the solution to this problem succinctly.

The Hunter

The time finally came for Chiumbo to become a man. However, it was not a happy occasion, for he faced his rite of passage with fear and trepidation. The expectation for young Kenyan warriors in his Maasai tribe was to hunt down a lion and cut off its tail. A daunting task even for the bravest adults.

Fresh in his mind was last years' mauling of his brother Okello. While Chiumbo wanted to show bravery and courage, he did not want to suffer the same fate as his brother. Gakuru would know what to do.

"Elder Gakuru, you have seen many boys become men, and you have also seen many fail. What must I do to be successful?"

"Young Chiumbo, meet me at the watering hole before sunrise, and I will show you what you must do.

While it was yet dark, the old warrior met the timid boy by the banks of the pond.

"Ok Chiumbo, pretend that I am the lion, and come get my tail."

With all the cunning craftiness he could muster, the wannabe warrior charged at the elder on the right side, and on the left. No matter how he attacked, Gakuru could turn his body and, if he were a real lion, would make mincemeat of the boy. Speed didn't matter – the experience elder could hear the footsteps of the boy, and pivot in time to stop him.

After it became apparent to them both that Chiumbo would not be able to succeed with any of the tricks he had in his arsenal, he finally gave up and sat down, dismayed.

"Rest, young warrior, and then I will show you my secret."

When the young man renewed strength, Gakuru told him to walk out into the plains, and return as a lion in search of a drink of water. Chiumbo acknowledged his command, and in several minutes returned as a thirsty lion. Not knowing what would happen, he slowed his gate to a laggard crawl on all fours and sought refuge beneath the lone tree at the watering hole. He peered hesitatingly around the trunk but saw no sign of the elderly warrior.

After some time had passed and with no sign of Gakuru, the boy meandered toward the bank of the pond. Suddenly, the elderly warrior was on the boy's back, and he quickly cut a swatch of fabric from Chiumbo's rear loincloth and ran off. The boy did not know what hit him because it all happened so fast!

Later that day, young Chiumbo found the elder sitting in his tent, grinning from ear to ear.

"Elder Gakuru, why was it so easy to cut off my "tail," when you are not as fast or as strong as I am?"

"Young one, it's very simple. When you attack the lion on his level, facing him in the eye, you will surely lose because you are fighting him in his arena. I won because I hid in the tree and fought you from a different vantage point. You faced me, the lion, on my terms, but I changed my perspective."

CHAPTER 5

Perspective

A person stuck in a pit has tunnel vision. The only thing you can see from your vantage point in a pit is what happens directly above you. You're not able to survey your domain. You only have limited information about what's going on.

Chances are, even if you're on top of a mountain right now, your hands touched the sides of the cold, damp pit at some point in your life. It doesn't matter what put you there, you have sat in that place, and the old children's song starts playing through your head, "Nobody likes me, everybody hates me, I think I'll go eat worms…"

The thing about a pit is this – it's all a matter of perspective. When you survey your landscape, and all you see is darkness, then despair begins to take hold. You don't desire it, but it's an all too willing companion to make you believe that there's no way out. And even if you put yourself in the pit because you were hiding from another problem, you begin to feel like you've backed yourself into a corner, and you have no hope of escaping.

One of my favorite movies is The African Queen with Katherine Hepburn and Humphrey Bogart. There is a scene in the movie, where their boat runs aground, and drinking water dries up. Once the viewer is sufficiently convinced that their demise is imminent, it begins to rain. The two near-death protagonists are so exhausted and close to death that they just lay there in the boat awaiting their doom. But then the movie cuts to a sunny day, and the camera begins to pan out. As it does, you see the lake just on the other side of a few bushes, and you realize that the rain caused the water to rise and propelled them towards their destination. In just under a minute, your perspective has changed from watching two people perish to watching hope arise and believing that they can make it after all.

For myself, when it comes to some of my vices like eating too many sweets and junk food, or not exercising consistently, I give up too easily. I'll do good for a few weeks; then, I'll see that Hot sign flashing at Krispy Kreme, and it's all over. Or I'll stay up late catching up on tv shows I have missed, and I'll be too tired to get my workout in because it's more convenient to stay in bed. What an ugly spiral. You may not deal with food the way I do, but there's probably a few things that you feel drag you down into this pit.

In 2 Kings 6, the servant of the Prophet Elisha found himself in a sticky situation, and it wasn't at all his fault. The king of Aram was at war with Israel and was trying to set an ambush, but Israel kept finding out about this plan. Of course, word got back to the King of Aram that Elisha was warning the King of Israel of these plans as the Lord would reveal them to him. So, troops traveled to Dothan to dispose of this holy man, and that is where we join this story in verse 15:

"Early in the morning a servant of the Holy Man got up and went out. Surprise! Horses and chariots surrounding the city! The young man exclaimed, "Oh, master! What shall we do? He said, "Don't worry about it – there are more on our side than on their side." Then Elisha prayed, "O God, open his eyes and let him see." The eyes of the young man were opened, and he saw. A wonder! The whole mountainside full of horses and chariots of fire surrounding Elisha!"

2 Kings 6:15-17 The Message

When we're wallowing in our pit of despair, we could certainly use a little perspective. In Star Wars: The Empire Strikes Back, Master Yoda told Luke that he must unlearn what he had learned to use the force. I'm sure you're perfect, but for me, I get in the habit of looking at things only through my physical eyes and forget that there is a Spiritual realm with real angels and demons. I forget about the horses and chariots of fire. I forget about the cloud of witnesses that went before me and encountered the same problems. I find myself adding fuel to the fire of my pain and self-loathing because it has a loud voice rather than put a megaphone up to my Bible app and blare the answer to my problems from the Word.

Changing perspective sounds easy in theory, but the implementation is where it gets tricky.

That's paramount to telling the 77th Infantry Division during the Battle of Okinawa that all they need to do is secure Hacksaw Ridge. Sure, we'll scale this wall while the Japanese are shooting us off the ledge from their established position. That sounds easy! Simple plan – we're down here, and all we need to do is get up there and take out all the soldiers that the 96th failed to get.

If you aren't familiar with the story of Hacksaw Ridge, it's worth looking at the life of Desmond Doss, the famous Seventh Day Adventist who rescued nearly one hundred men within the span of a couple days. With bullets narrowly missing him, Desmond dragged the wounded and deceased soldiers that fell in battle to the side of the ridge and lowered them down single-handedly with a rope harness he designed. With fatigue setting in, he kept praying, "Lord, help me get one more. Just one more Lord."

I can see a picture of this battle in my mind. His commanding officer had ordered the retreat after so many casualties, but Desmond looked and saw the wounded crying out for help. The rest of his platoon retreated and were safely back at base, but Desmond just continued to bring body after body and lower them down from his new vantage point. The rest retreated to the comfort and safety of the hole, but Desmond could hear the crack of the whip on the chariots of the angel armies surrounding him. God was on his side, and nothing else mattered if he was doing the Lord's will.

Besides the inherent benefits we receive from moving from the hole to the hilltop, there are many reasons to get out of our funk and live in the fullness of what God intends for us. His intentions are imprinted securely in His last words before He arose into heaven: "Go therefore and make disciples of all the nations, baptizing them in the name of the Father and of the Son and of the Holy Spirit, teaching them to observe all things that I have commanded you; and lo, I am with you always, even to the end of the age." Amen. Matthew 28:19-20 NKJV

While it's important to have an amazing relationship with our Father God in worship, it's vital that we know there's more to life than our wants, our desires, and our needs. God created us to be conduits of grace to the people we meet. Jesus told his followers that they were the light of the world. He went further when He stated that no one could see your light hidden under a basket. Only on a lampstand can your light shine. Only on a hill will it bring light to a dark city. My friend, aside from connecting with our Creator, we must get out of the pit so we can help others. If we change our perspective, we see our value to others as the connection to God's healing, hope, and help.

Nothing but God's grace and the power of the Holy Spirit can draw us into communion with the Father, but there is something therapeutic and healing that happens when we point others to Jesus love. There have been times on missions' trips and ministry events that I did not want to lead the worship or preach a message. My energy was gone, and I retreated to my cave of self-loathing. But something happened when I pushed through and obeyed the Lord. My healing came through seeing others set free and delivered. The light I shined in other's dark places also illuminated my heart.

I would describe myself as a techie. If the latest and greatest iPhone comes out, I want in. 4K TV with HDR? Yes, please! Last Star Wars movie involving the original cast? I'll be there opening night dressed as Chewbacca. Ok, everything but the Chewbacca part. But I'm sure you get what I mean – I'm a Gen Xer, but my tech consumption is more on par with a Millennial. So, imagine my horror when the internet went out at my house one Saturday recently. Internet, tv, and even printer are out! I had big plans for this Saturday – TV, surf the web, hang out on the couch. With my plans shot, I started to complain. I wallowed in my despair and self-pity. But then something happened.

I felt a call to my knees. When I turned off my whiny voice and got quiet, I could hear the Lord calling me to prayer. Finally, I relented and went to my War Room style prayer closet, and I began to intercede. If you're not familiar with this term, intercede, it is a request made for someone else. It's an unselfish prayer because you typically receive no benefit from it. And in this case, I didn't know who I was praying for, but I felt a strong burden to pray. I'm not sure how long I prayed, but I kept going until I felt the burden release.

By changing my perspective from whiny, overweight man who wants to sit on the couch and waste time to prayer closet prayer warrior, I radically altered my day! The time I spent pleading the blood of Jesus over someone I didn't know was time well spent. My actions stopped me from descending into my pit, and they reconnected me with the Creator. My problem with worship was solved by focusing on others.

If you find yourself in a pit, it's time to change your perspective. Becoming outward focused is one of the best ways I have found to change the viewpoint on my situation. The reason is because while we may not want to change for ourselves, because we don't think much of ourselves, we will change for a cause we believe in, namely fighting for others.

CHAPTER 6

Worship

You may say to yourself, "I'm in chapter 6 of a book on worship, and there's nothing in here about worship." Ok, sure, that's fair. But this book is about the worship crisis in our lives, and how to fix it. If you wanted a book that deep dives into the Hebrew words like Yadah, Towdah, Barak, Zamar, Halal, Shabach, or Tehillah, then you have unfortunately purchased the wrong book. Please call 1-800-SORRY-NOTSORRY for a full refund.

I think there are plenty of great resources that delve into the meaning of worship, and ways to do it. I don't think it's any secret that you can sing, dance, lift your hands, lay prostrate, play instruments, kneel, shout, etc. God crafted our ears to enjoy the sound of music, and our bodies to enjoy the rhythm of the beat. There are so many ways we can praise and worship our Lord.

To suggest that a particular expression of worship or the combination of all the forms shown in the Bible would solve your problems connecting with God would be a travesty. It's so amazing to be part of a diverse world full of cultural and familial differences that allow for all sorts of expressions in worship. There's not a "right" way to praise the Lord. You can't suggest that someone is going too heavy on their Yadah (lifting hands to heaven), and too light on their Shabach (a whole-hearted shout), and this is leading to their problem in worship.

By its very definition, worship is an intimate connection between the worshipper – us – and the worshipee – the Lord. The expression you use in your worship anywhere apart from a congregational setting is between you and God. There are times to shout, and there are times to kneel. There are times to extend your hands towards heaven or to remain silent in reverence and awe. Don't allow someone's personal preferences to dictate how you worship. Otherwise, you'll start to compare any lack of intimacy with God with the expression of worship. And if you've assumed that God only hears you when you shout, you will associate that with true worship. If someone told you that you must raise your hands, or else God won't see your surrender, you might have a distorted view of your relationship.

I know people who enjoy raising their hands, and they feel close to the Father when they extend their hands to Heaven. Because of their personal experience, they develop a view of intimacy with God that occurs when hands reach towards the Creator. And if that expression becomes their go-to, then express away! But we know what happens in church – if someone else is having problems with worship intimacy, then the problem must be that they are not lifting their hands. If they lifted their hands, they would feel the same closeness. The danger is, not only is there no Biblical proof that it would solve this other person's problem, we have now reduced the beauty of our uniqueness down to one expression of worship. Couldn't a person achieve intimacy in worship through kneeling? Or shouting? Or dancing? Or even by Halal, which is a Hebrew word for praise, that means to be clamorously foolish?

When I'm leading worship, I do my best to allow worshippers to express themselves to God in a way that achieves intimacy for them. Most of us know that we can dance, shout, kneel, or be clamorously foolish, but we stick to singing or raising our hands. Good news, for those who want to get out of their comfort zone, but both hands raised is just a little too far, it's Towdah. It's like Yadah (raising both hands), but you only have to raise the right hand. It loosely translates as a handshake to seal an agreement. The point of this is simple – don't be swayed by someone who tries to tell you how to worship. But, be open to the Holy Spirit, guiding you to a place of intimacy.

King David is the go-to authority on worship. He was a prolific songwriter who spent hours alone in nature, tending to the flocks. Acts 13 and 1 Samuel 13 describe him as a man after God's own heart. What stands out from the Psalms is how raw and real David is with his songs. In Psalms 42 & 43, he asks himself three times, "Why are you cast down, O my soul?" I guess all that time out in the field with you, and the sheep can cause you to start talking to yourself. Good thing, he answered himself correctly! "I will put my hope in God! I will praise him again – my Savior and my God!"

Notice here that the answer came, not because of the expression he used in worship, but the attitude he established in his heart. Reducing our intimacy in worship down to the hand or foot gestures we use misses a more important Biblical truth of what we say with our mouth. David understood this, and it is the centerpiece of the Psalms. Please don't infer from this statement that our expressions of praise from our bodies aren't important! King Solomon said it best when he stated: "To everything there is a season, A time for every purpose under heaven." Eccl. 3:1 NKJV

Are there times in worship when you should dance? Yes. Are there times where you should lay prostrate before the Lord? Yes. Are there times to be clamorously foolish? Of course. But I'm not the one to tell you when those times should occur. The more you connect with God in your times of devotion, the more you will understand when and where to express yourself to Him. I will say this – if all the people in church are spending a moment of quiet worship to God, it's probably not the time to shout. But, if you're in a corporate worship service and everyone is dancing or shouting, this may be a good opportunity to jump in and get out of your comfort zone. Sometimes we allow our pride and fear of humiliation to get in the way of God trying to free us from something.

I remember sitting on the right side of the stage for a service when I was in Bible College. This change was already out of the norm for me since I usually sat on the left. Of course, I did this so I could sit by a girl. As the music started to heat up, and a spirit of freedom hit the place, I felt like God wanted to free me from things torturing my mind. I noticed that some people were dancing, and several were running a victory lap around the building. I resisted and kept resisting. There was a girl beside me that I was trying to impress! But, in that room, with the loud music, I heard God speak to my spirit – "Jesse, do you want to be free? Does it matter how freedom comes?" And then I knew what I had to do, but my flesh was still resisting. I said out loud, "OK, Lord," and I took off.

I can't imagine what this looked like to others! In my spirit, I was telling God that I wanted to be free, but my flesh was fighting the idea. In my spirit, I said to God that I would run a victory lap around the congregation with the others to declare my victory over the battle in my mind. But my body had other plans. My feet moved, but they refused to run. I ended up hopping a lap around the sanctuary like a bunny. Jesus' words rang true for me when He told the disciples, "The spirit indeed is willing, but the flesh is weak." My flesh felt foolish, but my spirit was free!

Now, if you're reading this and not of the full-gospel, charismatic persuasion, you may think I'm a nutcase for bunny hopping in church. But I would ask that you keep an open mind to what the Word says, rather than what your church experience has been. It would be a shame to get to Heaven and find that you missed out on walking in freedom in an area of your life because a denominational preference or societal queue got in the way. Remember, we are trying to fix the issues we have that block us from intimacy with God.

Taking Time

Drawing close to God does not have to live in a box. There is no perfect expression of praise or worship that creates intimacy every time, but it would do most people good to explore Biblical ways to worship that are outside their wheelhouse or comfort zone. The attitude and expectation we have during worship directs our words, which is the ultimate form of communication. God loves to hear His children express themselves to Him. But none of this will create a long-lasting relationship if we don't take the time to be in His presence.

There is no substitute for time. We are all given the same amount, but how we choose to spend it is up to us. No one else can work on our relationship with God for us. We can ask someone to pray for us for something, but their prayers do not cause us to go deeper in our relationship. I can ask my secretary at work to call clients and work on things that grow my business, and it can indirectly help my family through the money produced, but it does not strengthen or deepen my relationship with my wife. My relationship is directly impacted by the amount of time I spend with her.

Many spouses have found this to be true – every dollar in the world won't strengthen our relationship if I never spend time with her. There is no substitute for time. You may be able to farm out your responsibilities at work to grow a business, but a business is not a living, breathing human being. It has no emotional quotient. It only loves you when it's thriving. Your business will not hold you and comfort you when everything goes belly up. But the way some people treat their businesses in comparison to their families, you would think that they had found their soulmate.

No, there is no substitute for time spent in the presence. Can I get real for a minute? Maybe I should have put this at the beginning of the book – If you're only spending time worshiping God for a 20-minute worship set on Sunday Mornings, and you don't know why you are having problems connecting with God – you have identified the problem. Try holding together a marriage on a 20-minute conversation a week.

Long-distance calls haven't always been free. Anyone with me in the 40+ crowd can remember calling cards and AT&T's 'Reach out and touch someone' campaign. Julie and I didn't get married until January 3, 2004. We met in 1999 at Bible College but didn't start dating seriously until 2001. We were in separate states the whole time. There were several nights that we racked up huge bills talking because we couldn't help ourselves. I remember one bill that stuck in my mind the most - $414! Some people say you can't put a price tag on love, but my $414 bill says otherwise.

The reason we spent so much time talking on the phone is because we had no other way to communicate. Yes, there was the occasional Skype call when I upgraded from dial-up to DSL, but we had to coordinate plugging our computers in, etc. It was a whole thing. We wanted to know each other. And, if we were going to get married, we wanted to be sure we had found the right person. We had an advantage that others didn't – our only choice was to talk to each other. It's not much of a conversation if no one says anything! Distance forced us to communicate.

If you know the heart of God, you know that He pursued us long before we ever cared to know Him. He wants to know us even more than we want to know Him. Jesus told His disciples that He was going to prepare a place for them in Heaven. God has been preparing for us before we were born. He knows everything about us and is interested in us. He wants to spend time with us. You could say that the relationship is one-sided because God's thoughts and intents towards us are higher, better, greater, and grander than our thoughts could ever be towards Him.

However, as our Creator, God knows this about us because He created us in His image and likeness. Because of grace and Jesus' sacrifice, it's possible to become a Christian and go to Heaven without taking the time to know God, but what a travesty that would be on our part. We have the greatest gift available after salvation – the ability to communicate with the Almighty. But this requires our time. How much time do we dedicate and devote to this relationship after the 1-2-hour sacrifice on Sundays? Do we spend any time throughout the week sitting at His feet, or are we expecting the Sunday service to satisfy our need to connect with God?

When you boil it down, people make time for people or things that they love. A new relationship. A new hobby. An old hobby. Dining at a favorite restaurant. Whatever it might be that you love, you will make time for it. Let's say a man loves his wife, but he also loves watching sports – he may get tired because he will find a way to spend time with his wife but stay up late watching the games he recorded. It's possible to do both, but there is a price to pay.

How much do you want to know the Lord? How good do you want your relationship to be? Only the time you spend with Him will deepen the relationship. Yes, there is a difference in time wasted and quality time, but you never waste time when pursuing a deeper relationship with the Father. It's one thing to feel a disconnect in worship and your prayer life, but you will never fix this problem by avoiding God. He's omniscient and omnipresent. As we said earlier in this book, there is nowhere you can go to avoid God. He will pursue you until your last breath.

So, commit today to a deeper relationship by creating time. Time spent pursuing the things of God is time invested in your eternity. No one gets to the end of their life and says, "My life would have been complete if I had only binged on watching all 12 seasons of the latest fad show on Netflix." There is no show, hobby, or even human relationship that could ever compare with the eternal nature of our relationship with God. Begin with a 5-5-5 plan if you don't know where else to start. That's 5 minutes of Bible reading, 5 minutes of prayer, and 5 minutes of worship. Watch how even that small amount of time each day will ignite a new fire and passion in your heart.

CHAPTER 7

Fasting

In the modern church, I can think of no Spiritual practice less utilized by Christians than that of fasting. However, there are numerous verses in both the Old and New Testaments that speak on fasting. Before we start this chapter, I would like to turn your attention to Jesus' famous Sermon on the Mount. In 15 minutes, Jesus delivered one of the most powerful messages of all time. Notice three of the most powerful "When" statements in scripture:

Matthew 6:3-18 NIV says, "'But when you give to the needy, do not let your left hand know what your right hand is doing, so that your giving may be in secret. Then your Father, who sees what is done in secret, will reward you.

"And when you pray, do not be like the hypocrites, for they love to pray standing in the synagogues and on the street corners to be seen by others. Truly I tell you, they have received their reward in full. But when you pray, go into your room, close the door and pray to your Father, who is unseen. Then your Father, who sees what is done in secret, will reward you. And when you pray, do not keep on babbling like pagans, for they think they will be heard because of their many words. Do not be like them, for your Father knows what you need before you ask him.

"This, then, is how you should pray:

"'Our Father in heaven,
hallowed be your name,
your kingdom come,
your will be done,
    on earth as it is in heaven.
Give us today our daily bread.
And forgive us our debts,
    as we also have forgiven our debtors.
And lead us not into temptation,
    but deliver us from the evil one.'

For if you forgive other people when they sin against you, your heavenly Father will also forgive you. But if you do not forgive others their sins, your Father will not forgive your sins.

"When you fast, do not look somber as the hypocrites do, for they disfigure their faces to show others they are fasting. Truly I tell you, they have received their reward in full. But when you fast, put oil on your head and wash your face, so that it will not be obvious to others that you are fasting, but only to your Father, who is unseen; and your Father, who sees what is done in secret, will reward you."'

I realize that this passage has been in the Bible for nearly 2,000 years, so countless people have already noticed the pattern, but when I saw the word WHEN repeated three times here, it was a huge revelation to me. It's also amazing how God revealed it to me during a 3-day fast! How cool is that?

The problem with the argument "The New Testament doesn't mention fasting much, so we don't have to fast today," is that it's both unscriptural and simply not true. In fact, in this passage, Jesus lists three things that He assumed all believers would continue to do. Give, pray, and fast. Money, meditation, and mouth. Not multiple choice, it's all the above. And just because we as Christians don't want to fast because it's pretty much the most miserable thing on the planet, doesn't mean we shouldn't make it a regular part of our lives.

I've never been great at fasting because I love to eat food and consume. Even when it comes to media, I'm the guy with a laptop open, iPhone in one hand, iPad on my left, and notifications coming up on my Apple Watch at the same time. I listen to podcasts at 1.5x – 2.0x the regular speed so I can pack more into a shorter amount of time. The side effects of this lifestyle are an overweight middle-aged man with the attention span of a hummingbird.

I'm not the go-to authority on fasting. A 4-day fast with water and juice only is the longest I've ever gone. I read about these super-spiritual people who have 40-day fasts under their belt and wonder how they do it! Food is my kryptonite. One time I walked past a Krispy Kreme doughnut shop, and when the smell entered my nostrils, I gained 5 lbs. Ok, not really, but it sure felt like it.

Don't take my advice on fasting because I said it. I wrote this book so you could break free from bondage in worship. Using fasting to break bondage over our lives, as well as others, works because Jesus said it works, not because Jesse wrote it in a book. To ignore the meat of this next verse could leave you stuck in a rut with God. Some things can only change in the Spirit realm through fasting, coupled with prayer. Notice what Jesus said to His disciples when they couldn't cast a demon out of a man:

Then the disciples came to Jesus privately and said, "Why could we not cast it out?"

So Jesus said to them, "Because of your unbelief; for assuredly, I say to you, if you have faith as a mustard seed, you will say to this mountain, 'Move from here to there,' and it will move; and nothing will be impossible for you. However, this kind does not go out except by prayer and fasting." Matthew 17:19-21 NKJV

They could not cast out the demon because they didn't add fasting to their prayer. Jesus didn't say this to make them feel bad. He defended His disciples when John the Baptist's disciples came to ask why they did not fast. His explanation? Simply that a time was coming when they would fast to mourn the loss of their Savior, but not while He was on the earth with them.

Jentezen Franklin is a pastor of a large, multi-site church in Georgia. I both admire him and consider him an authority on fasting. He has made it a regular discipline in his life, and it shows through his sermons, his church, and his life. In his book, The Fasting Edge, he says, "Prayer and fasting were a big part of Jesus's life. Why should it be such a small part of yours? If Jesus needed to fast, how much greater is our need to fast?"

In another book by Franklin called Fasting: Opening the Door to a Deeper, More Intimate, More Powerful Relationship with God, he wrote: "We must get to the place where we are desperate for God again. We must begin to desire Him more than food or drink. Let us be filled with the Bread of Life instead of the refuse of religion. Begin to make fasting a regular discipline and see how God answers your hunger!"

Our worship is simply the praise and adoration we offer up to God as a sacrifice. I can think of no greater sacrifice than going without food. I remember when I was a car salesman, and I went for ten days without selling a single car. In frustration, I told God that I wasn't going to eat until I sold a car because I needed to feed my family. Amazingly, I sold a car that day. When I told my manager what I had done, he, as a non-Christian, noted that a lack of food is the absolute strongest motivator on the planet.

Fasting is powerful. There are many natural health benefits associated with the practice, but I'm focused on the Spiritual benefits. Denying your body the food it craves, and instead pouring the Word of God into your soul, and praying for wisdom, clarity, and direction is the best way I can see from Scripture to get back on track. We drift away because we hide from God. We can't hear God speaking to us because we become selfish and callous to His voice. Too many things have invaded our space, and God becomes distant.

Denying the craving for food is like stepping out of your body as your spirit man, taking your body, holding it up against a wall, and saying, "Snap out of it! Get it together, man! You don't control me. You are subject to a higher authority." Left to its own devices, our flesh will rule every part of our lives. When I look back at my failures, it's easy to have 20/20 vision now and see that my spirit was not in control – my selfish desires had free reign.

When you fast, your spirit connects with The Spirit, and while your body may be miserable, you are fulfilling a God-honoring command. Not a command in the sense that you get under condemnation if you don't complete a 40-day fast, but simply an expectation that God has of His children to grow into adulthood as Christians. The fast isn't for Jesus' benefit; it's for us.

Every major leader in the Bible fasted. Moses, Elijah, Paul, Jesus, Esther, Ezra, and many more. I'm sure it affected them just as it affects you and me.

We don't like to fast. But the important question to ask yourself is this: "Is temporary discomfort valuable enough to win a Spiritual battle against the enemy?"

It will take grit and determination to finish a 3- day fast. It will take incredible tenacity to get to 7 days. I can't imagine how someone could make it 40 days on just water and juice because I've never done it. But, in my last 3-day fast, I heard the Lord speak to me to come away more often and spend time with Him. I have set in my heart to fast every month, not every year. I want to know the secrets that God has for His children. If certain demons only come out by prayer and fasting, then I want to be prayed-up and fasted-up so that I'm ready for anything the devil may try to bring.

Hiding from God and people, the hurts and pains and agony we deal with may hinder our worship but fasting can break it. Many people don't need another sermon or worship service to draw them deeper; they need to act. There isn't a book on this planet that can help you land your dream job if you never apply for said job. There isn't a sane man in the world that would marry a woman that won't leave her house, or talk, or visit. For some things, the only answer is action! Dreaming about college won't help you graduate college; you must put in the hours and the work. The first two letters of God's name are G-O, but yet we sit back and wait.

There are deep truths and spiritual secrets that unlock only by fasting. If there were another way, someone would have found it by now! Yet we don't fast because our bodies tell us that we will die. The hunt for survival kicks in and our flesh begins to make plans for our funeral. As a fellow terrible faster, I'm here to tell you something very powerful in your life. When this happens, go to a mirror and shout at the top of your lungs, "Shut up flesh! You don't tell me what to do!" Mic drop.

Decide today to fast. Plan it. Gather a list of prayer requests, and make sure other people are on your list. Read a book or two on fasting. Maybe your goal is one day. Maybe 3. Maybe you are a pro, and you can go for seven days or longer. Maybe you want to do a Daniel fast of meats and sweets. Look, all you've got to lose is a couple pounds – the upside is infinitely better.

CHAPTER 8

Knowing

There was once a Shakespearean actor who was known everywhere for his one-person shows of readings and recitations from the classics. He would always end his performance with a dramatic reading of Psalm 23.

Each night, without exception, as the actor began his recitation - "The Lord is my Shepherd, I shall not want." The crowd would listen attentively. And then, after the Psalm, they would rise in thunderous applause in appreciation of the actor's incredible ability to bring the verse to life.

But one night, just before the actor was to offer his customary recital of Psalm 23, a young man from the audience spoke up. "Sir, tonight, do you mind if I recite Psalm 23?" The actor was quite taken back by this unusual request, but he allowed the young man to come forward and stand front and center on the stage to recite the Psalm, knowing that the ability of this unskilled youth would be no match for his talent.

With a soft voice, the young man began to recite the words of the Psalm. When he finished, there was no applause. There was no standing ovation as on other nights. The only sound in the room was the sound of weeping. The young man's recitation had so moved the audience that every eye was full of tears. Amazed by what he had heard, the actor said to the youth, "I don't understand. I have been performing Psalm 23 for years. I have a lifetime of experience and training - but I have never been able to move an audience as you have tonight. Tell me, what is your secret?"

The young man quietly replied, "Well, sir, you know the Psalm... I know the Shepherd."

Do you know God, or do you know about God? God knows us intimately, and He wants us to know Him. Hebrews 4:15 NKJV says, "For we do not have a High Priest who cannot sympathize with our weaknesses, but was in all points tempted as we are, yet without sin." Our God knows us.

In Isaiah 53:3 NIV, the prophet foretells our Savior's plight on this earth, when it says that, "He was despised and rejected by mankind, a man of suffering, and familiar with pain. Like one from whom people hide their faces, he was despised, and we held him in low esteem." As you and I struggle to connect with God on a personal level, we need to understand what kind of God we serve. According to this verse, he wouldn't have had many Facebook followers or Instagram likes. But, He came…for us. Jesus willingly came down for us to be despised and rejected.

Sometimes the jolt of electricity we need to ignite our times of worship is a little perspective on what Jesus did. How can we adequately worship someone when we don't know about their character or their sacrifice? Yes, most Christians know about Easter, and they know that Jesus came to die for their sins. But do we somehow separate Jesus of the Godhead, and look at Him and His sacrifice as something completely different than what God the Father did by sending Him? Do we forget that Jesus said, "My Father and I are one."?

Jesus also said that if anyone has seen Him, they have seen the Father. If we are going to solve our problems in worship, we must see God the Father through the redemption of Jesus. Yes, Jesus paid the price of admission, but He did so to a good God who loves us enough to sacrifice His Son. We also must acknowledge the role the Holy Spirit plays in our everyday life. Jesus may be the key to our atonement and salvation, but there are three parts to the Trinity, and they operate as One God.

Whether you are a firm believer in three separate members of the Trinity, or you belong to the camp of Oneness doctrine which says that it's one God only, you have to acknowledge that God loves humankind with an unconditional love. I see points from both sides, and as a trinitarian, I strongly believe we must view God, Jesus, and the Holy Spirit as distinct and co-equal.

For example, if we don't allow the Holy Spirit to lead us, guide us, help us, walk with us, or use us, then we begin to see God as a far-off deity, uninterested in the affairs of humans. Jesus knew this about people, and that's why He told us that He was going to prepare a place for us, but He was sending a Comforter to come alongside us, and not only be with us, but who would be in us. The Holy Spirit takes the connection directly from God the Father and places it inside our human spirits to establish a direct connection.

The problem with stating that The Lord your God is One God and ignoring the many other verses in the Bible that show Him as Father, Son, and Holy Spirit, you will begin to see Him as impersonal and distant. God is the most personal being on the planet because He formed you, crafted you, and designed you with a purpose in mind.

I'm not against college degrees, or education, if we don't educate ourselves out of the blessings of scripture. Some theologians have spent many hours in the Word, and none on their knees. If you're having trouble connecting with God in worship, spend as much time in the presence of God as you do in the pages of His Word. I can't see how someone could miss the point of the love letter from God to humanity called the Bible, but if God's love for you isn't coming alive through the pages, then it also needs to be quickened to your spirit in the presence of God.

You are at a disadvantage to me, most likely. You probably didn't have a praying mom. Maybe you did, but she wasn't as great as my mom. I was able to not only read through the Bible with my family many times as I grew up, but I saw my mom rise before dawn, and pray for our family, as well as many other prayer requests. I believe it was my mother's prayers that kept me from getting too far off track. I'm not saying I had a perfect life – far from it – but there were many obstacles and entanglements I could have ended up in had it not been for my mom.

When I saw my mom on her knees in our laundry room, praying for Dan and me, it brought the scripture to life. My little brother Dan is an amazing man of God, and I'm proud to have him close by. Sure, Dan hit a rough patch along the way, but so did I. Sometimes, I think back to those times, and I know that I had a mom praying for us so that we would come back.

Prayers of faith help us see God as an ever-present help. If we never see God as loving and listening to our cry, then He will remain distant and foreign to us. Our view of God must come into line with the Word to connect with Him. When I heard my mom pray those prayers for us and many others, I saw her faith in action. And when I saw those prayers get answered, I knew that God wanted to a part of my life daily.

To critics who may say, "I prayed for healing for my brother, but then he died." I would say this:

please don't let a terrible, horrible experience with prayer rob you out of future blessings. I don't have all the answers, and I don't know why your brother died, but I do know that healing is for the church today, because the Word says it is, and because I've experienced it. I have laid hands on the sick and have seen then miraculously healed. I have seen people walk into a service with their head down, and with a cloud of gloom resting on them, leave the service with the joy of the Lord.

We can't let one experience skew our view of God for the rest of our lives. I was talking with someone one time, and they mentioned one cell phone carrier that they used to be with and said that they were never going to use them again. I asked them why not, and it, as it usually does in these cases, boiled down to one bad phone call with a customer service agent. Their view of a company that employs thousands of people across the nation and the world, and has the highest customer service ratings of any of the wireless carriers, was summed up in one bad experience with one person in one call center on one day in one hour. But now, because of their experience, they were the worst of all time.

Furthermore, their problem was that the company had charged them roaming charges. It was completely in their right to do so. This individual thought that the charges were too high, even though they signed a contract that said otherwise. But the company was the problem...sure.

James, the brother of Jesus, said that sometimes we don't get the things we pray for because we ask amiss, not believing that we will receive our request. The Apostle Peter said that when husbands don't honor their wives, it could hinder their prayers. None of us know every situation, but we must acknowledge that there could be reasons why prayers don't always get answered or in the way we expect them. We can't allow every personal situation to change the way we see God.

When we change our perspective towards God to see Him as loving towards us, and personal, then it will radically alter the way we worship Him. Knowing who God is to us is key to our relationship. I don't think anyone understood this relationship more than the Apostle John, whom Jesus entrusted with His mother. When John was between 80-95 years old, he penned these words from the Holy Spirit: "Whoever confesses that Jesus is the Son of God, God abides in him, and he in God. And we have known and believed the love that God has for us. God is love, and he who abides in love abides in God, and God in him." 1 John 4:15-16 KJV

To truly abide with God, it's a daily communion with Him. It's looking at the mountains, and the rivers and trees, and thanking God for the beauty in nature. It's looking at our spouse, or our kids, and realizing that God put amazing creativity and thought into crafting these people that make up our families. Worship is not something we do or accomplish; it's living in constant communion with a personal God who created and designed us for His pleasure.

CHAPTER 9

Enemy

B e sober, be vigilant; because your adversary the devil walks about like a roaring lion, seeking whom he may devour. 1 Peter 5:8 NKJV

The first time I remember an experience with the devil was after watching a special on the assassination of JFK on tv with my parents at age ten or so. For several months after this, I was terrified of mirrors. Every time I walked past a mirror, a spirit of fear gripped me. I was worried something was going to jump out at me, or there was something inside of me that would come out when I saw the mirror. It was a completely irrational fear, and it had no grounding in the TV special and was not related to any physical rationale. It was demonic. Knowing the Word of God like I do now, there was no doubt that a demon was trying to torture me. Yes, I was a Christian who belonged to a Christian household, but at that time, I did not know my authority as a Christian to overcome the devil. I was in bondage.

Demonic bondage is not to be confused with being demon-possessed. I see no scripture that supports the idea that a demon could control a Christian. I do see verses that Peter and Paul wrote to the church to be on the lookout for the activities of satan.

For a ten-year-old baby Christian, my fear of mirrors for a season was a powerful tool used by the devil to keep me in constant terror. It controlled where I walked in my house to the point that I found myself pre-closing doors to bathrooms so I wouldn't have to see the reflection as I walked by. The greatest weapon that satan uses against Christians is fear because if fear grips your heart, you won't exercise your faith.

It's important to understand the enemy. Knowing who our enemy is will help us to understand how to fight and resist him when he tries to deceive us. Notice what Jesus said to the Pharisees and Sadducees that were trying to kill him:

"Jesus told them, "If God were your Father, you would love me, because I have come to you from God. I am not here on my own, but he sent me. Why can't you understand what I am saying? It's because you can't even hear me! For you are the children of your father the devil, and you love to do the evil things he does. He was a murderer from the beginning. He has always hated the truth, because there is no truth in him. When he lies, it is consistent with his character; for he is a liar and the father of lies. So, when I tell the truth, you just naturally don't believe me!" John 8:42-45 NLT

What we can glean from this are the tricks the devil uses against us. First, the devil is a murderer. That's his number one ploy. Don't tell me that the 54 million-plus babies aborted in the US since 1973 isn't a scheme of satan to take out innocent life before it begins. I don't care what your politics are – you cannot find a shred of evidence in the Word of God that backs up any argument other than a child's right to life. Murder is the devil's M.O., and he has deceived many into separating humans and fetuses, and somehow everything changes once the baby leaves a birth canal. It's a lie.

In a later passage, John states again that the enemy comes to steal, kill, and destroy. There's no way to sugarcoat this. We live in a world where euthanasia is around the corner, partial-birth abortion is law, and the sanctity of life has become an old-fashioned idea. The devil is behind it all. He has blinded the eyes of many good people from the truth because he can't afford to have an army of on-fire, powerful Christians rise and keep him at bay. Satan is a murderer. And he manufacturers lies to pull it off.

Another way that the enemy ruins your relationship with God is through unforgiveness. Paul told the church at Corinth to forgive others, lest satan should take advantage of us; for we are not ignorant of his devices. 1 Cor 2:11 NKJV

When a root of bitterness goes down into your soul, it begins to choke the life right out of you. The other person is usually oblivious to your pain or rage, but you are locked in a cell of agony and torment because of the evil things you begin to think about them. Nothing will ruin your relationship with God faster than your hatred and unforgiveness toward another person created by God. In the heat of the moment, we may think they are an awful person, but some of our problems with others are just the result of a misunderstanding.

If you had 100 drivers in a room, only 49 are technically above-average drivers. And if you considered the top 10% great drivers, that means only ten people in the room are great. Yet studies show that 80% of people on the road believe they are above average. I can speak authoritatively on this point because I was licensed in the state of Ohio to teach both classroom and behind the wheel driver education classes. I saw firsthand the cocky 16-year-olds that needed experience but thought that they were the experts.

Don't worry; I have a point with my segue into driving statistics. When you compare road rage and anger behind the wheel with someone stuck in a prison of unforgiveness, you will find many similarities. Both people feel they are justified in their actions because the other person is in the wrong. Both are angry about an action someone took towards them. Both are in a heightened state of frenzy because of what someone else did. Neither the person with road rage nor the person who refuses to forgive can see anything they did wrong. All the blame lies with someone else.

And that's the heart of the issue. If we see unforgiveness as a trick of the enemy to enslave and trap us, then we will know how to fight it when we see the root begin to grow in our lives. I suppose it's a fair question to wonder why our beef with someone would interfere with our relationship with God. Maybe now that I'm a father of two kids, and maybe because I grew up with two siblings, I have some perspective on this.

Good parents love both of their kids. We don't allow one kid to disrespect the other or fight the other. We teach them to love each other because they are both our children, and we want the very best for them. No good parent would allow one kid to bully their other kid, teaching them a lesson. Neither will God stand for one person to act in rage towards another person, because they are both His creation. It doesn't matter if one has professed Jesus as Savior and Lord, and the other has not, because God hand-crafted each of them.

When that dirty old deceiver comes along and sees that he can drive a wedge of unforgiveness between two people, he will take the opportunity every time! Whenever two people are fighting, and in strife, I imagine these little demonic imps sitting around, throwing a party. Evil has won. You must recognize unforgiveness as a tool of the enemy so you will know how to respond when the opportunity arises.

Of all the tactics the devil uses, they find their root in deception. When John the Revelator describes the 1,000-year binding of satan, in Revelation 20:1-3, notice what he says about him:

Then I saw an angel coming down from heaven, having the key to the bottomless pit and a great chain in his hand. He laid hold of the dragon, that serpent of old, who is the Devil and Satan, and bound him for a thousand years; and he cast him into the bottomless pit, and shut him up, and set a seal on him, so that he should deceive the nations no more till the thousand years were finished.

Satan's tricks all boil down to one thing: deception. He will prey on people, especially those who haven't renewed their minds. I can look back on times where I did not have as much control over my thought life as I should have. It's easy to see the lies and deception that the deceiver whispered in my ear. You're not good enough. You're not holy enough. If God loved you so much, why didn't He grow your church? If you were a better Christian, God wouldn't allow this to happen to you.

We must be aware of the lies that the devil will use against us. They are the same for all people. Satan's lies are simply the exact opposite of what the Bible says about us. If the Bible says we are a new creation – old things have passed away, and all things have become new, then what do you think the devil will tell us? Maybe you're not saved because you yelled at your wife, kicked the dog, and wasted all the money God gave you.

The devil will use the lie of salvation by works most often to Christians, because if he can get us to think that our redemption is worthless and based on our good deeds, then he can keep us from doing anything great for God. If we don't see this as a lie, then we will remain in bondage, and the devil has won a small victory. We are still on our way to heaven, but we may not help anyone else get there. When Satan can't take us out completely, he'll settle for a smaller victory of stunted spiritual growth.

My teenage years were the 90s. And in my youth group, we were shown a video called Hells Bells: The Dangers of Rock 'N Roll. While this film is old and outdated now, I can see what the producers were trying to do. They targeted certain groups of singers and musicians that specifically used satanic imagery and words in their music videos and tried to warn unsuspecting kids in youth groups to stay away from these bands. Of course, they probably didn't realize the unintended side effect of exposing sheltered Christian kids to bands their parents would never let them listen to anyway. I'm not saying I'm one of those kids, but I did find myself searching for a little Black Sabbath or AC/DC after watching the video.

This book is not a debate about what music a Christian should listen to, but rather a guide on how to live with an open window from our heart to our Father God. Let's get real for a minute – music is powerful, and some songs can hinder our walk with God. No, not every secular song is evil, and no, not every Christian song is Bible-based or theologically sound. That's why we are to keep our guard up.

A few years back, I was in a clothing store in the mall, and a song came on the radio. It was popular at the time, and it was on commercials and movie trailers on tv. All of a sudden, without realizing it, I started to groove a little, as the words came out of my mouth, "It's getting hot in here, I wanna take my clothes off, It is, getting so hot, I wanna take my clothes off…" What? Wait a minute; I don't want to take my clothes off! Nobody in this department store wants to see that! When the devil uses music, he makes it easy as pie for us to sing out things we would never think about saying.

When I was a full-time youth pastor, teens argued with me for years that they listen to the music for the beat, not the words. Bunk and bologna! If I played the top 40 list to teens in America, 90% of them would start singing along. Words matter, the devil knows this, and if he can get teens to sing some sexualized, physical, profanity-laced, surface-level love songs, then he can destroy the most important institution we have for a cohesive society – marriage. Look at the stats – it's working. Only 29% of Americans age 18-34 were married in 2018, compared to 59% in 1978. Plus, the number of couples living together has tripled in that same period. Some of the blame for this must go to the music.

To keep a watchful eye out for satan doesn't

mean we are looking behind every bush or every corner, it means we recognize when he steals from us, kills our dreams, or destroys our lives. His only game is deception, but Jesus wants to deliver us. We recognize the devil when things disappear. God doesn't take things from you – He gave His only Son that you might have eternal life.

If you're experiencing distance in your times of worship, take stock of your life, and begin to identify situations crafted by the deceiver to steal from you. The greatest theft he will commit is stealing your time. He'll use any means necessary to keep you sick, discouraged, and bound up, so you feel like you have no time for Bible study, for your family, or general life enjoyment. The devil will get you to think that it would be better for Jesus to take you to Heaven now, so you don't have to endure this life any longer. Unfortunately, this works on many people – the devil has deceived them into thinking that no one wants them, especially not God.

Recognize the lie today.

Take back your life.

You are important and valuable!

Your family needs you.

The world needs you.

Jesus loves you.

Satan hates you.

The best thing you can do to take authority over satan when his attacks start is to remind him what a little piece of dung he is. The Bible says to humble yourself before God, resist the devil, and he will flee. I put on the armor of God found in Ephesians 6, and then I start talking to that foul, disgusting creature that Jesus cast out of Heaven. Here's an outline:

"Devil, you have no authority in my home. God cast you and 1/3 of the angels out of heaven, and you are a defeated foe. When Jesus went down to the pit for three days, he arose with resurrection power in His hands, as well as the keys to death, hell, and the grave. He gave authority to the church, which includes me. You have no power over me or my family. Get your stinkin' hands off me, my finances, and my house. Go back to hell where you came from and leave me alone!"

You can use whatever scriptures you would like when you speak to that foul turd. My editor thinks I should capitalize satan and the devil, but he is a defeated enemy, and not worthy of me even holding down the shift key. You need to treat the devil from the vantage point as victor to regain victory in your life. Begin to say what the Bible says about him, and that action will remove his power from your circumstances. You will have to do this over and over, but it will work.

CHAPTER 10

Music

If you were expecting a manual on how to worship, I'm sorry to disappoint you. There are many good books on the types of worship, how to enter the presence of God, and how to sit at the Master's feet. These are all great ideas and worthy of putting in your spirit, but we also must deal with things that hinder our worship. Discouragement, pride, the devil, hiding, not fasting – these are all things that can hinder our times of worship.

Let's talk about a touchy subject for some – music and lyrics. We all have our favorite artists, songs, and style of music. That's great! I have been in times of worship with some headbanging teens who love God with their whole heart, and love to express how they feel to him in a way that some would think foolish and undignified. I've also had my heart touched in nursing homes singing hymns to people often forgotten. I've never felt God in country-western music, but I know many that have. (Please, no letters about how wonderful country music is. I will file them in my trash can.)

Because there is no direct instruction in the Bible on what style is most holy, I don't see that as a distinction worth debating. There are still some in church who believe drums and electric guitars are the work of satan, but there's no scripture that backs this up.

There is, however, plenty of scriptures that talk about the power of your words and what you say. We touched on this in the last chapter, but there is more to this issue than the devil prompting artists to write satanic or sexually charged songs. There are songs we sing at church that appeal more to our souls' feelings, rather than focus on God's power to help us. Some songs make Christians sound weak, anemic, and barely able to hold it together. Still, other songs glorify the problem more than the problem-solver.

I will try not to stomp on your modern favorites, except to say, please run them through a Biblical filter. God can still get glory from new believers singing from their heart to God, even if the words are wrong. But there is a place of maturity that Christians arrive at where we must judge and filter the things we say or sing. Liking the catchy melody or driving beat isn't enough to overcome unscriptural lyrics.

Let me give an example of an old song that hopefully won't ruin too many people's favorite song. Charley Pride wrote a song called, Lord, Build Me A Cabin in Glory, and I want to look at the lyrics on the chorus:

Yes, build me just a cabin in the corner of glory land
In the shade of the tree of life that it may ever stand;
Where I can just hear the angels sing, and shake Jesus' hand
Lord, build me a cabin in the corner of gloryland
Blessed Lord, I'm not asking to live in the midst
For I know I'm not worthy of such splendor as this
But I'm asking for mercy while humbly I stand
Lord, build me a cabin in the corner of gloryland

There's no doubt that Pride was trying to be humble here – the song is sincere. But the question is, does it hold up to scripture? Notice what Jesus said to His disciples in John 14:2 NKJV: In My Father's house are many mansions; if it were not so, I would have told you. I go to prepare a place for you."

The NIV translation says, "There is plenty of room for you…" So, Jesus not only went to prepare a place for us; there's plenty of room there! Plus, once Jesus has made us free, we are free indeed. There's no Biblical evidence that some will get cabins, and others will receive mansions. We do know that there will be no lamps or darkness in heaven because God is the light. The only grading system we know of is how it relates to the crowns we will receive. It may sound humble to ask for just a little piece of land way back in the corner to build a shack, but it doesn't hold up to scriptural scrutiny.

The goal of this chapter isn't to pick apart every song we sing on Sundays, but rather, to run them through the lens of the Word of God. When a new believer is growing, I believe that God treats their spiritual growth the same way we treat the growth of our children. We don't expect our kindergartners to use proper pronunciation, correct spelling, or four-syllable words. We do expect our college student children to learn on pace with a college education. Our relationship with God is the same because we reflect His glory.

I encourage you to step back, take a good look at what you're singing and feeding on. There have been many times as a worship leader that I have had to either correct the theology of a song or leave it out of my church. Car-ride Karaoke with Jesse experienced the same transformation. No beat or melody on earth will hinder my relationship with God. You may think this is a small matter, but I encourage you to hold your belief system up to the light of the Word. Jesus didn't mince words when He told his disciples, "If your hand causes you to stumble, cut it off. It is better for you to enter life maimed than with two hands to go into hell, where the fire never goes out. And if your foot causes you to stumble, cut it off. It is better for you to enter life crippled than to have two feet and be thrown into hell. And if your eye causes you to stumble, pluck it out. It is better for you to enter the kingdom of God with one eye than to have two eyes and be thrown into hell." Mark 9:43-47 NIV

I guess you could also apply this message to your ears – I mean, Peter didn't mind cutting off an ear! All kidding aside, the issue here isn't about legalism, it's about spiritual growth. What are you willing to change to achieve freedom in your worship? What are you willing to put up with to protect your intimacy with the Father?

Are lyrics a big deal? I believe they are. I believe a Biblically sound worship set at church is as important as a Biblically sound sermon prepared by the minister. Depending on the type of church you go to, this can also differ as widely as the theology of a Baptist church vs. a Pentecostal church. So, another question could be, who is right when it comes to being Biblically sound.

Well, that's a very deep question, and I'm glad you asked. The root of the question is if words are important in song lyrics, how do I know I'm saying the right words? My denomination does not believe in ______, so should I remove all songs that talk about ______?

Let's be honest; if we're long-term Christians, we have probably settled into a set of beliefs. If you believe differently than me on what I call the "finer points" of the Christian faith, it's going to be hard for either one of us to convince the other to adjust and change our philosophy. And I'm ok with that. If we are sincerely trying to work out our salvation with fear and trembling, God will honor that.

There is a principle in scripture established by

Jesus when He spoke to the Samaritan woman at the well, that will illuminate a perspective on this. Looking at John 4:19-24 NIV, we see the interaction between them:

"Sir," the woman said, "I can see that you are a prophet. Our ancestors worshiped on this mountain, but you Jews claim that the place where we must worship is in Jerusalem."

"Woman," Jesus replied, "believe me, a time is coming when you will worship the Father neither on this mountain nor in Jerusalem. You Samaritans worship what you do not know; we worship what we do know, for salvation is from the Jews. Yet a time is coming and has now come when the true worshipers will worship the Father in the Spirit and truth, for they are the kind of worshipers the Father seeks. God is spirit, and his worshipers must worship in the Spirit and in truth."

The keyword here is truth. Without sounding trite, the Christian walk focuses on Relationship, not Religion. Jesus foretold His death, burial, and resurrection in not so many words, through His explanation of worship. The way to connect with God is through our spirits to the Spirit. But what we say is vitally important. It must be truthful.

It's a powerful saying – the truth will set you free! Are you worshiping God in spirit and truth? We call out to God and ask Him why He feels distant as He whispers back to us, "Are you telling me the truth?" For spoken truth to be active, alive, and powerful, we must believe it. For too long, many of us have lied to ourselves.

So, how does this connect to our worship songs? Jesse, this seems like a long rabbit trail. Well, I'm so glad you asked again. The point is that we must line up the words we speak and the words we sing, with the beliefs we hold in our hearts. Confusion comes when we expect the sermon to be Biblically sound and in line with our beliefs, but not the song service.

For example, if you have decided that God no longer miraculously heals today (I hope you don't believe this), and miracles passed away with the disciples, then you have a belief formed in you. Right or wrong scripturally, we are not going to debate this. But we can agree that either from the church you attend or the denominational stance you affirm, healing is no longer a promise to Christians.

But, on Sunday, Worship Pastor Johnny B Good sings out the words, "I believe, You're my healer..." And because of the power of music, you find yourself singing this song. But you begin to feel uneasy. Something's not right, but you can't put your finger on it. Was the key too high? Why couldn't I enter into worship this morning? The questions roll through your mind like a Times' Square marquee.

In this example, we see a contrast of song lyrics being incompatible with a belief. Now, I'm not suggesting that you comb through all your worship songs, so you set up a meeting with your worship leader to point out the dogmatic inconsistencies.

I do think it's wise to assess what your singing to make sure it's truthful.

Before you label me a "live your truth" nutjob, please don't think I'm suggesting that there is no such thing as absolute truth. Certain views in the Bible are essential to Christianity – Salvation by grace, Infallibility of Scripture, Forgiveness of sins, Heaven and hell, to name a few. However, a subject like Eschatology, which is the study of end-time events like the Second Coming of Christ, is open to wide interpretation. There are very good, sincere people who believe that Jesus is coming before the tribulation period, and just as good, sincere people, who think that Jesus will come after the tribulation. Neither position will affect our atonement through Christ, or our entry into Heaven.

So, while the non-essential doctrine will not determine our salvation, it still shapes who we are and how we view the world. It's still important. I would argue that if you have songs that discuss pre-tribulation, healing, the believer's authority in Christ, speaking in tongues, or any other doctrine that doesn't directly affect your relationship with Christ, you need to decide if it measures up to the theological position you expect from the pulpit.

I remember the first couple of weeks after Julie and I were married. I was living in the church parsonage as the youth pastor, and so Julie moved in with me. We started our life together after dating long-distance. We were in our mid-20s, so there were routines, meals, bedtimes, and so much more to work out.

One thing Julie found out about me was that when I got home, I liked to take my shoes and socks off, and set them wherever they ended up in the living room. It could be days before those shoes made it back to my closet. In fact, by the end of a week, there may be 4-5 pairs of shoes and corresponding socks laid out across the room. And this was a convenient situation because you don't have to go back to the bedroom to wear another pair in the mornings, and the socks that didn't smell too bad could find a second life. The argument, "This cuts down on our water bill," was not valid in Julie's opinion. Neither was the idea that a living room could double as a closet! In several months, many other habits of mine would turn up as we grew to know each other.

The foundation of marriage is mutual love and adoration for one another. Julie and I had that in spades. However, the habits and customs, parenting styles, Bible studies, driving habits, and all the other "finer points" of marriage are up to interpretation, and continual evolution as life happens. We never compromise our essential values, but rather our non-essential proclivities.

For me, I could decide to take a hardline on my socks and shoes in the living room, and if I had, I could have had the house to myself once again. My love for Julie was stronger than my love for shoes and socks in the living room. I know I made the right choice.

In my quiet time with the Lord, there are songs that I have cut out because they don't line up with my beliefs. However, in a public worship service, I'm not suggesting that you don't sing just because the song isn't fully theologically in line with your beliefs, but recognize what truth is and what it isn't.

Think about this – words matter. The writer of Hebrews said in chapter 11 that "the worlds were framed by the word of God…" If God's Word can frame worlds, and we, as the disciples of Jesus, have been given authority to tread on snakes and scorpions, and on all the power of the enemy, then understand that what we sing has the power to create and the power to tear down.

Just like my example with my socks and shoes, many of us have beliefs and thoughts that took root years ago. Maybe they were planted by our parents, or the Bible, or a preacher, or a college class – however they came, the things that took root form our belief system. So, I would challenge you with this: Do your beliefs line up with the Bible, or do they bring you off track?

Just because you are a worrier because your mom or dad taught you the fine art of panic, doesn't mean you have to be, or that you can't change. Just because you believe that all men are dogs because the last three have treated you that way doesn't make it true. In the Apostle Paul's second letter to Timothy, he admonished the younger pastor to study so he could rightly divide the word of truth. We have the same admonition to run our beliefs and thoughts through the filter of the Word. I would argue that this applies to the songs that move our feet and run through our soul.

CHAPTER 11

Communion

One of the most powerful disciplines we experience as Christians is the sacrament of communion. This act of worship precisely centers us and reminds us of Christ's sacrifice. The Apostle Paul described this command succinctly when he wrote his first letter to the church at Corinth:

For I received from the Lord Himself that [instruction] which I passed on to you, that the Lord Jesus on the night in which He was betrayed took bread; and when He had given thanks, He broke it and said, "This is (represents) My body, which is [offered as a sacrifice] for you. Do this in [affectionate] remembrance of Me." In the same way, after supper He took the cup, saying, "This cup is the new covenant [ratified and established] in My blood; do this, as often as you drink it, in [affectionate] remembrance of Me." For every time you eat this bread and drink this cup, you are [symbolically] proclaiming [the fact of] the Lord's death until He comes [again]. 1 Corinthians 11:23-26 AMP

In this passage, Paul is encouraging the church to continue this practice. While he writes to a church here, we don't see Jesus partaking in communion only at church. The first time that Jesus introduced communion to His disciples was in the upper room. After they finished their meal, He passed the bread and the cup around, charging them to remember His sacrifice. Not in a church service, but an upper room of a house.

Religion and religious practices have a way of robbing our joy and our relationship with God. Isn't it amazing how we associate communion only with a church building, yet Jesus' only examples are outside the church? Certainly, we should take communion at church as Paul told the Corinthians, but to limit this experience to the "4 walls" was never God's intention.

When I was on staff at a church in Alaska, I was part of a pastor's prayer network that met weekly. It was so great to pray and believe God for our city with other men and women of God from various denominations and backgrounds. Each week, one person would give a short devotional from each of the 35 churches represented.

One week, a woman who co-pastored a church with her husband, walked up to the podium with a package of Ritz crackers, and Big Red soda. As she gave scriptures and personal experiences demonstrating the power of communion, she then opened the soda and crackers to disperse to the crowd. Her point was simple – the power of communion was not in the type of bread, or whether someone used grape juice or wine, but rather the remembrance of the body and blood of the Lord. She also encouraged us to remember more often, and in private settings with our families, how important it is to thank the Lord for His sacrifice until He comes.

The example of Big Red and Ritz crackers is indelibly etched in my brain, and I will never forget her illustration. My eyes were opened that day, just like the two men on the road to Emmaus. In fact, in Luke 24, when Jesus walks with two devout men and explains who the Messiah is throughout scripture, they remain clueless. Remember, Jesus has already risen from the dead and is walking around in His glorified body. There was no social media, or 24-hour news cycle running for them to recognize him by His appearance.

But when Jesus broke bread and handed it to them, suddenly, their eyes were opened, and they recognized Him! We need more suddenly's in our lives! There is power that comes when we partake in communion, and it opens our eyes to things of the Spirit.

I don't believe you could over-remember the Lord's death until He comes. If you want to take communion every morning, nothing is preventing you from doing that. If the motivation is to keep a constant reminder of the powerful sacrifice He made for us, then it has power in our lives. The moment that communion becomes routine or religious, it loses the enlightenment that God intended.

Bring communion into your personal life. Take it with your family. Partake in the elements before you spend time singing and praising God and watch how your spirit absorbs the things of God.

CHAPTER 12

Unwritten

Our brains cannot comprehend God's love and forgiveness. We know that when He forgives us, he casts our sins in depths of the sea! Christ's forgiveness towards us canceled the weight of sin that was against us. Nothing will free us more than receiving the revelation from God that He forgave us! The truth that we've been made righteous, holy, and blameless in the sight of God should be enough to keep us free. But we must walk in this freedom. We must walk out our salvation before God.

A major theme of this book is the fact that we go into hiding when we feel shame. The root is unforgiveness. We hide from God because we are unable to forgive ourselves. We hide from others because we are angry and unforgiving towards them, or because we feel like they could never forgive us for what we've done.

What's amazing is that this gift of Salvation – God wiping our debt clean – is still the issue we deal with the most. Only, we say we believe it, but the devil and our circumstances whip us, and beat us, and enslave us again to the taskmaster of unforgiveness. Understanding and recognizing this pattern in our lives is the first step to freedom.

There's even more great news – applying the principles of this book will open the Heavens in your life immediately. Jesus likened the Body of Christ to a bride on her wedding day. It may be hard for the guys reading this to relate, but everyone would agree that a wedding day should be one of the happiest days of a person's life. (If it's not, then perhaps you should run from the altar, not walk down the aisle).

Jesus has already done the work to make you clean, right, and holy. Now the onus is on us to walk in new life. Romans 6:4 KJV says, "Therefore we are buried with him by baptism into death: that like as Christ was raised up from the dead by the glory of the Father, even so we also should walk in newness of life." The way we fix our problem with worship is by acting like Jesus did what He did. He paid the price, but sometimes we don't act like it. We act like God forgot us. He knows the hairs on our head, and I would venture to say on our back and in our ears as well. Men included. Does that sound like someone who abandoned you? Does that sound like someone who forgot about you?

I told you personal stories from my life so you

could see my struggles and understand that we all deal with issues. But that chapter of my life is already in the annals of time. That is my history, not my future. The rest of our lives are the unwritten chapter.

When the devil begins to remind you of your past, then begin to remind him of his future. When the consequences of your mistakes begin to rear their ugly heads, don't let them define who you are. Those pages are written – the life ahead of you is ready for your new story. Change the plot and redefine your story.

While I attempted to provide a comprehensive list of ways to reconnect with God in worship, it will never cover every person's story. If you find freedom in worship by another means than one covered in this book, would you send me an email? I would love to know how God is writing His story in your life! My email address is jesse@jessedmiller.com

Worshiping God should be the best part of our Christian experience because He gets our praise, but we get His presence. The Bible says that in His presence is fullness of joy. I encourage you today to take time and get alone with God. Forget the concerts, forget the conferences – the hype you experience will only last a season. The power of God you feel when it's you and Him cannot be replicated in a stadium or a corporate setting. How intimate can a married couple be in public before someone shouts, "Get a room!"

If you are alone with God for 5 minutes and you don't feel anything, don't give up! I've never been a prolific writer, but I've felt God stirring me to encourage people to press on in His presence through writing and teaching. I rarely sit at the keyboard and feel the words flow through my fingers. One time I sat for an hour before typing a word because I wanted to get God's thoughts in my spirit first. Sometimes you will have to stir up the presence and get yourself in an attitude where your mind is quiet, and you can communicate with the Lord. We do this by praying, singing in our language, and singing in the Spirit. We kneel, raise hands, lay prostrate, or any other iteration of praise that is appropriate for us and the moment. Hebrews 4 talks about laboring to enter the rest. Don't be afraid to get your hands dirty because the reward is great!

Let's end with Psalm 150 NIV. There is always a place, always a time, always an instrument, and always a reason to praise God!

Praise the Lord.

Praise God in his sanctuary;
  Praise him in his mighty heavens.
Praise him for his acts of power;
  Praise him for his surpassing greatness.
Praise him with the sounding of the trumpet,
  praise him with the harp and lyre,
praise him with timbrel and dancing,
  praise him with the strings and pipe,
praise him with the clash of cymbals,
  praise him with resounding cymbals.

Let everything that has breath praise the Lord.
Praise the Lord.

ABOUT THE AUTHOR

Jesse Miller

Jesse is an author, speaker, pastor, and blogger. He resides in Prescott, AZ with his wife Julie, his kids Abigail and Benjamin, and their dog, Stella. 

BOOKS BY THIS AUTHOR

Red Letter Ministry

In this book, churches and ministries can associate themselves to Jesus' style of ministry and the way He interacted with and preached to: Those who hated Him Those who loved Him His disciples The young The sick It also examines the style of communication that Jesus practiced and how it can be used in a modern context to deliver parables, sermons, encouragement and rebukes, while organizing groups of people, from the multitude right down to a single person. Jesus had his own inimitable style when it came to preaching the word of God. Somehow and somewhere along the line we lost that. Now, matching that unmistakeable passion that He had for others, Red Letter Ministry aims to help you to rediscover it.

www.ingramcontent.com/pod-product-compliance
Lightning Source LLC
Chambersburg PA
CBHW062229150726
47991CB00006B/2495